The Numbers:
Calories, BMI, and Portion Sizes

Mason Crest
450 Parkway Drive, Suite D
Broomall, PA 19008
www.masoncrest.com

Printed and bound in the United States of America.

First printing
9 8 7 6 5 4 3 2 1

Series ISBN: 978-1-4222-2874-6
ISBN: 978-1-4222-2883-8
ebook ISBN: 978-1-4222-8945-7

The Library of Congress has cataloged the
    hardcopy format(s) as follows:

        Library of Congress Cataloging-in-Publication Data

Crockett, Kyle A.
  The numbers : calories, BMI, and portion sizes / Kyle A. Crockett.
    pages cm. – (Understanding nutrition: a gateway to physical & mental health)
  Audience: 10.
  Audience: Grade 4 to 6.
  ISBN 978-1-4222-2883-8 (hardcover) – ISBN 978-1-4222-2874-6 (series) – ISBN 978-1-4222-8945-7 (ebook)
  1. Food–Composition–Juvenile literature. 2. Diet–Juvenile literature. 3. Food–Caloric content–Juvenile literature. 4. Food portions–Juvenile literature. I. Title.
  TX551.C79 2014
  664'.7–dc23
                        2013009809

Produced by Vestal Creative Services.
www.vestalcreative.com

UNDERSTANDING NUTRITION
A GATEWAY TO PHYSICAL & MENTAL HEALTH

The Numbers:
Calories, BMI, and Portion Sizes

KYLE A. CROCKETT

Mason Crest

CONTENTS

INTRODUCTION

by Dr. Joshua Borus

There are many decisions to make about food. Almost everyone wants to "eat healthy"—but what does that really mean? What is the "right" amount of food and what is a "normal" portion size? Do I need sports drinks if I'm an athlete—or is water okay? Are all "organic" foods healthy? Getting reliable information about nutrition can be confusing. All sorts of restaurants and food makers spend billions of dollars trying to get you to buy their products, often by implying that a food is "good for you" or "healthy." Food packaging has unbiased, standardized nutrition labels, but if you don't know what to look for, they can be hard to understand. Magazine articles and the Internet seem to always have information about the latest fad diets or new "superfoods" but little information you can trust. Finally, everyone's parents, friends, and family have their own views on what is healthy. How are you supposed to make good decisions with all this information when you don't know how to interpret it?

The goal of this series is to arm you with information to help separate what is healthy from not healthy. The books in the series will help you think about things like proper portion size and how eating well can help you stay healthy, improve your mood, and manage your weight. These books will also help you take action. They will let you know some of the changes you can make to keep healthy and how to compare eating options.

Keep in mind a few broad rules:

- First, healthy eating is a lifelong process. Learning to try new foods, preparing foods in healthy ways, and focusing on the big picture are essential parts of that process. Almost no one can keep on a very restrictive diet for a long time or entirely cut out certain groups of foods, so it's best to figure out how to eat healthy in a way that's realistic for you by making a number of small changes.

- Second, a lot of healthy eating hasn't really changed much over the years and isn't that complicated once you know what to look for. The core of a healthy diet is still eating reasonable portions at regular meals. This should be mostly fruits and vegetables, reasonable amounts of proteins, and lots of whole grains, with few fried foods or extra fats. "Junk food" and sweets also have their place—they taste good and have a role in celebrations and other happy events—but they aren't meant to be a cornerstone of your diet!

- Third, avoid drinks with calories in them, beverages like sodas, iced tea, and most juices. Try to make your liquid intake all water and you'll be better off.

- Fourth, eating shouldn't be done mindlessly. Often people will munch while they watch TV or play games because it's something to do or because they're bored rather then because they are hungry. This can lead to lots of extra food intake, which usually isn't healthy. If you are eating, pay attention, so that you are enjoying what you eat and aware of your intake.

- Finally, eating is just one part of the equation. Exercise every day is the other part. Ideally, do an activity that makes you sweat and gets your heart beating fast for an hour a day—but even making small decisions like taking stairs instead of elevators or walking home from school instead of driving make a difference.

After you read this book, don't stop. Find out more about healthy eating. Choosemyplate.gov is a great Internet resource from the U.S. government that can be trusted to give good information; www.hsph.harvard.edu/nutritionsource is a webpage from the Harvard School of Public Health where scientists sort through all the data about food and nutrition and distill it into easy-to-understand messages. Your doctor or nurse can also help you learn more about making good decisions. You might also want to meet with a nutritionist to get more information about healthy living.

Food plays an important role in social events, informs our cultural heritage and traditions, and is an important part of our daily lives. It's not just how we fuel our bodies; it's also but how we nourish our spirit. Learn how to make good eating decisions and build healthy eating habits—and you'll have increased long-term health, both physically and psychologically.

So get started now!

1

The Numbers Behind the Food We Eat

Have you ever wondered why you have to learn math? Well, you can use math when you eat!

Numbers and math are one way to understand nutrition. Choosing what to eat and how to be healthy can be hard to remember. Numbers give us a way to keep track of everything, from how much food we eat to how much we weigh.

Nutrition Facts

Serving Size   1 Cup (53g/1.9 oz.)

Servings Per Container   About 8

Amount Per Serving

Calories 190	Calories from Fat 25

% Daily Value*

Total Fat 3g	**5%**
Saturated Fat 0g	**0%**
Trans Fat 0g	
Cholesterol 0mg	**0%**
Sodium 100mg	**4%**
Potassium 300mg	**9%**
Total Carbohydrate 37g	**12%**

Checking the labels on the food you eat is the best way to find out how many calories are in the food, what ingredients the food is made with, and how much of your daily value of different nutrients the food gives you.

What Is Good Nutrition?

Nutrition is all the ways a person **consumes** food. Nutrition involves what kinds of food you eat, how often you eat it, and how much you eat.

Good nutrition means healthy eating. In general, someone with good nutrition eats healthy foods, eats an **appropriate** amount of food, and eats at least three full meals a day.

Everyone should be interested in good nutrition! Making healthy food choices makes you feel better and helps your body work better. In the long run, good nutrition keeps you healthy and prevents serious sicknesses.

Of course, the opposite of good nutrition is poor nutrition. Eating unhealthy foods, eating too much or too little, and skipping meals or eating too many are part of poor nutrition.

Poor nutrition leads to lots of health problems. Sometimes unhealthy food choices make you feel **bloated**, give you a headache, or put you in a bad mood. Over time, poor nutrition leads to weight gain, heart problems, **stroke**, **diabetes**, and more.

Good nutrition is a good goal to have. You don't have to make the healthiest food choices every single time you eat, but you should try to generally eat well. Choose healthy

What Does Consume Mean?

When someone **consumes** something, he eats it.

What Does Appropriate Mean?

Appropriate means what's right and fitting.

What Does Feeling Bloated Mean?

When people say they feel **bloated**, they mean that their bodies feel puffy and swollen. They feel like they're suddenly fatter than they really are. Their clothes may fit more tightly than usual, or the rings on their fingers may be tighter.

What Is a Stroke?

When people say that someone had a **stroke**, they mean that the blood flow inside the person's brain was interrupted for some reason. When this happens, brain cells die. Afterward, the person may not be able to speak or move normally. If too many brain cells are killed, the person will die.

What's Diabetes?

Diabetes is a disease in which the body can't use sugar the way it should. Diabetes is tied to being overweight.

foods most of the time, don't skip meals, and eat just until you're full. Numbers can help you figure out just how to do that.

Food Label Numbers

So how are you supposed to keep track of what's healthy and what's not? Use numbers! Numbers can help you understand the part of food called nutrients. Nutrients are substances our bodies can't make, but which they need to work right. We eat food to get the nutrients we need.

Vitamins and **minerals** are nutrients. **Carbohydrates**, fats, and **protein** are other nutrients. Food has all of those nutrients. Healthy foods have lots of the nutrients we need.

People only need tiny amounts of some nutrients. Sugar and salt are two examples. The body needs a little bit of each to work right. But people tend to eat too much sugar and salt. For instance, soda has a lot of sugar, and chips have a lot of salt. Too much of those nutrients cause health problems. Foods with too much of them are unhealthy. Unfortunately, lots of people eat lots of sugary and salty foods.

Scientists have figured out ways to measure just how many nutrients foods have. You can use websites to look up the foods you normally eat to see how many nutrients they have. Or you could use food labels.

Food labels are a handy way to check up on the numbers that tell you how many nutrients a food has and if it's healthy or not. You'll find food labels on just about every food with a package. Look for a black and white chart with a whole bunch of numbers.

Notice that each nutrient has a number right next to it. Those numbers are the actual amounts of the nutrient in one serving of that food. The food company decides how much a serving is. One serving might be a granola bar, or ten crackers, or one cup of broccoli. The package of food might have a lot of servings, but the numbers on the food label are based on just one serving.

The amounts of nutrients are given in grams or milligrams. One gram weighs about as much as a paperclip. A milligram is lighter, and weighs about the same as a snowflake.

The really important numbers are on the right side, though. Each nutrient also has a **percent** by it, on the right. The percents are called daily values.

You need 100 percent of each nutrient every day to be at your healthiest. Daily values tell you how close you are to getting 100 percent of each nutrient.

Let's take calcium. Suppose you're drinking some milk. You check the food label and see that one serving size is 8 ounces. You measure and discover that's exactly how much you're drinking in your glass. Those 8 ounces have 30 percent of your daily value of calcium. That's a lot! You'll need 70 percent more during the rest of the day, though, to get up to 100 percent. You might get that from drinking another 2 glasses of milk (which would get you up to 90 percent), and then having some cheese, or even a little bit of ice cream to give you your last 10 percent.

What Are Vitamins and Minerals?

Vitamins and **minerals** are both types of nutrients. Plants and animals make vitamins. Minerals come from dirt and water. Plants and animals can't make minerals. But plants do suck them up from the dirt and water, and animals eat them. Then we eat the plants and animals, so we get the minerals too.

What Are Carbohydrates and Protein?

Carbohydrates are starchy foods, like bread, cereal, and pasta. Carbohydrates give our bodies energy. **Protein** is found in meat, beans, and nuts. It helps build muscle.

What's a Percent?

A **percent** means one in a hundred. One percent is one out of a hundred. Fifty percent is fifty out a hundred. If 87 percent of kids like carrots, that's another way of saying 87 out of 100 kids like them.

What Does Sensitive Mean?

When someone is **sensitive** about something, she is uncomfortable talking about it or gets upset about it easily.

Food labels also have a number called calories up at the top. Calories are important for your health. They tell you how much energy a food has. Chapter 2 will tell you a lot more about calories.

All in all, food labels and nutrition information can tell us if a food is healthy or not. With practice, you can figure out how healthy a food is just by looking at the numbers.

Numbers and Health

Weight is another important nutrition number. People can get very **sensitive** about their weight. But weight is just one measure of how healthy you are.

One magic weight doesn't exist. Different people are healthiest at different weights. A healthy weight is important for feeling your best and helping your body work well.

When you think about health, you can look at lots of different numbers. Here are just a few:

- How many hours of sleep do you get? People need between seven and nine hours normally. Getting fewer hours of sleep is not healthy.
- What is your blood pressure number? Blood pressure measures how much your blood is pushing on your arteries. Blood pressure has two numbers in it. A healthy blood pressure is usually around 120/80.

A Guide to Food Label Words

Food labels have so many words on them! Here's what they all mean:

Calories: A measure of how much energy a food has.

Calories from fat: How much of the food's energy comes from fat.

Serving size: A specific amount of the food. All the rest of the information is based on how much of each nutrient is found in that amount.

Servings per package: How many servings are in the entire container.

Total fat: All kinds of fats, both good and bad, measured together. (Fats are substances that keep skin and other organs healthy.)

Saturated fat: A kind of fat found in meat and dairy products. It's best to limit how much you eat of this kind of fat, because too much isn't good for you.

Unsaturated fat: A kind of fat found in vegetables and nuts. This is considered a healthy fat.

Trans fat: A kind of fat made in factories. Trans fat is not good for you.

Cholesterol: A kind of fat that comes from meat and dairy products. We need a little, but not a lot.

Sodium: Another name for salt. A little keeps the right amount of water in the body, but too much isn't healthy.

Carbohydrates: Starchy and sugary foods that provide your body with energy.

Sugar: A kind of carbohydrate that tastes sweet.

Dietary fiber: A kind of carbohydrate that keeps the digestive system healthy.

Protein: A nutrient that keeps muscles and blood healthy.

Vitamin A: A nutrient that keeps skin, teeth, and eyes healthy.

Vitamin C: A nutrient that helps the body repair itself when it is hurt.

Calcium: A mineral the body needs for strong bones.

Iron: A mineral that helps blood carry oxygen to the rest of the body.

Limit these nutrients

Get enough of these nutrients

Nutrition facts

Serving size 1 cup (9 oz - 255g)
Servings per container 2

Amount per serving
Calories 485　　　**Calories from fat 220**

	% Daily Value*
Total fat 1 oz - 28 g	**32%**
Satured fat 0.5 oz - 14g	38%
Trans fat 0.2 oz - 6g	
Sodium 0.03 oz - 0.9g	**13%**
Total carbohydrate 1.5 oz - 42g	**11%**
Dietary fiber 0 oz - 0g	0%
Sugars 0.2 oz - 6g	
Protein 0.2 oz - 6g	

Vitamin A	5%	Calcium	18%
Vitamin C	3%	Iron	6%

* Percent Daily Value are based on a 2500 calorie diet. Your Daily Value may be higher or lower depending on your calorie need.

Quick Guide to % Daily Value:

5% or less is low

20% or more is high

- How many minutes do you exercise every day? Doctors say young people should get at least sixty minutes of activity in every day. Walking to school, playing sports, or taking a swim all count.

What Does Lifestyle Mean?

Your **lifestyle** is the way you choose to live. A healthy lifestyle includes choosing to eat healthy foods, choosing to get enough sleep, and choosing to exercise.

All these numbers help you see how healthy you are. When one of those numbers isn't what it should be, you should consider making changes in your **lifestyle**. You might need to take medicines, eat healthier foods, or get more exercise. Talk to your doctor if you're concerned about any of these numbers.

2

Calories In
and Calories Out

Some people think calories are something to avoid. However, all people need calories, just like we need nutrients.

Measuring Energy

Calories are simply a measure of energy. They aren't good or bad. They're just a measurement.

All living things need energy to survive. For people and animals, food is how they get energy. All the food we eat has energy.

Energy is the main reason we eat food. Humans can't make their own energy to power themselves. Plants, on the other hand, get their energy from the sun and don't have to eat like we do.

Think of a car. You have to fill it with gas to keep it going. The gasoline provides the energy. Food provides energy for people, to keep us going.

Calories are the measurement of the energy in food. You could measure how much a piece of bread weighs in ounces. You could measure how wide it is in inches. You could also measure how much energy it has in calories.

Calories don't depend on how much foods weigh or how large the food is. They depend on how much energy is in them. A half-cup of peanuts—as many as would fit in your palm—has over 400 calories. A whole cup of chopped lettuce—a small salad's worth—has less than ten!

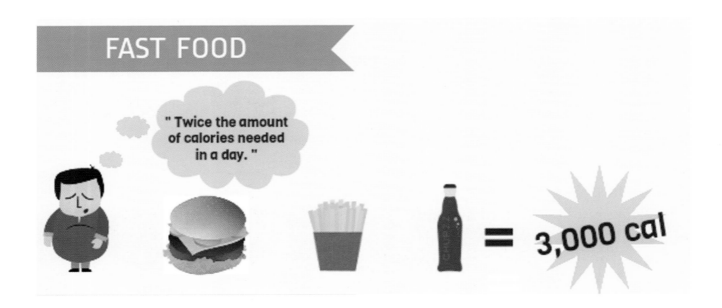

Many foods have more calories in them than you might think. A burger, fries, and soda from a fast-food restaurant could be thousands of calories in just one meal, many more than you need in a single day!

Taking in Calories

People need calories every day, but only a certain number of them. Most people need about 2,000 calories every day. Some people need more and some people need less. How many you need depends on whether you are male or female, your age, your weight, and how much exercise you get.

So how much food is 2,000 calories? You might think it's a lot, but it's probably less food than you think. One fast-food hamburger could be over 500 calories. Four hamburgers would equal a whole day's worth of calories. A bowl of cereal might have 150 calories. One banana has 100 calories. All the food you eat in a day should add up to about 2,000. So if you write down all the calories you eat in a day, at the end of the day, you just need to solve an addition problem to find out how many calories you've eaten.

The calories in all foods come with different nutrients. You generally want calories from foods with good nutrients, like healthy fats, protein, or vitamins and minerals. Unhealthy foods have calories that are from sugar, salt, or unhealthy fats. We only need a little bit of these nutrients. Too much of them causes health problems. Calories that are mostly from sugar, salt, or unhealthy fats are called empty calories.

Burning Up Calories

Our bodies use a lot of the calories we take in. Walking and moving around uses calories of energy. Breathing and pumping blood uses calories of energy. Even just thinking and sitting uses calories. The body is burning up calories every minute of the day and night.

The more you move your body, the more calories you need. Athletes and people who work out a lot need a lot more calories than people who don't do any exercise. Watching TV, for example, only burns about one calorie a minute. Dancing burns 4 or 5 calories a minute. So here are more math equations that will help you determine how many calories you're using if you watch television for an hour versus dancing for an hour.

1 calorie x 60 minutes = 60 calories burned in an hour of watching TV
5 calories x 60 minutes = 300 calories burned in an hour of dancing

Counting Calories in Nutrients

Different kinds of food have different calories. In fact, each kind of nutrient has a different number of calories. Protein, for example, is a nutrient that has four calories in every gram. If you were eating some cheese with seven grams of protein, you would be eating twenty-eight calories that came from protein.

7 grams protein x 4 calories per gram = 28 calories

Other calories in the cheese come from other nutrients.

Carbohydrates also have four calories per gram. Soda, for example, has a lot of sugar, which is a carbohydrate. One can of soda usually has around 40 grams of sugar. In all, there are 160 calories from that sugar.

40 grams sugar x 4 calories per gram = 160 calories

Soda doesn't have much else in it, so all the calories in it come from sugar.

Fat has the most calories per gram. Fat has nine calories for every gram. Half an avocado has about eleven grams of healthy, unsaturated fat. When you do the math, you see half an avocado has 99 calories.

11 grams of fat x 9 calories per gram = 99 calories

There's a big difference there!

Different people's bodies burn different amounts of calories too. People with more muscles use up calories faster. Men and boys usually need more calories than women and girls. Sometimes people's bodies just burn more calories because that's how their bodies work. Those people need to eat more. Do you know anyone who can eat and eat and always stays really thin? Her body probably naturally burns more calories than other people's.

Balancing Calories

To be at your healthiest, you must balance out how many calories go into your body and how many are burned up. When those numbers aren't balanced, you gain or lose weight, and you may get sick.

Eating too many calories and not burning up enough of them leads to weight gain. Remember, most people need about 2,000 calories to get through the day. Any more than that, and you start to gain weight. That's because your body stores energy in fat cells. The more fat cells you have, the heavier you'll weigh.

You can balance out eating extra calories by moving more. When you move more, you burn more calories. More intense activities burn more calories. Playing soccer for an hour will use up more calories than walking for an hour.

Eating too few calories or burning too many of them leads to weight loss. When you don't eat as many calories as you need, your body starts to use stored energy. The body slowly uses up the fat it has accumulated. People who exercise too much without eating more also end up losing weight.

Some people lose weight on purpose. People who are overweight can eat less or they can move more to lose weight. The best thing is to do both! Don't start a weight loss plan unless you really need one, though. Talk to a doctor to figure out if you need to lose (or gain) weight.

Balancing everything out can be like an experiment. Let's say you really like eating. You eat 2,500 calories every day, and you notice you're starting to gain weight. You want to stay healthy, so you start running a lot. After you've been running every day for a few

How Many Calories Do I Need?

Different people need different numbers of calories every day. Boys tend to need more than girls. And people who are more active need more than people who don't move around very much. Where do you fall? Ask your doctor to help you figure out if you need to be eating more or fewer calories. Here are some general guidelines:

Girls, 9–13 years old
Not very active: 1,600 calories
Sort of active: 1,600–2,000 calories
Very active: 1,800–2,200 calories

Girls, 14–18 old
Not very active: 1,800 calories
Sort of active: 2,000 calories
Very active: 2,400 calories

Boys, 9–13 years old
Not very active: 1,800 calories
Sort of active: 1,800–2,200 calories
Very active: 2,000–2,600 calories

Boys, 14–18 years old
Not very active: 2,200 calories
Sort of active: 2,400–2,800 calories
Very active: 2,800–3,200 calories

weeks, though, you start to feel really weak, and now you're losing weight too fast. You don't feel great. You realize you need to eat more because your body is burning so many calories while running. Now you actually have to eat more.

Listen to what your body is telling you. Don't eat when you're not hungry. Eat when you are hungry. Move around when you're feeling restless. Learn to pay attention to the messages your body sends you.

Pay attention to weight gain and loss too. You don't have to weigh yourself every day, but check the scales every once in a while. Are your clothes too tight, even though you haven't grown any taller? Or are they too loose? Your doctor is the best person to tell you whether you need to be eating more or fewer calories. Talk to her before you make any decisions.

How Much Is Too Much?

People gain weight for a lot of reasons. One reason is that most people tend to eat really big portions of food. Portions are the amount of food you choose to eat in one sitting.

The more food you eat, the more calories you're taking in. And all those calories lead to weight gain and other health problems. By understanding portions and keeping them under control, you can stay on top of your health!

Nutrition Facts

Serving Size: 1 Can

Amount Per Serving

Calories 150

	% Daily Value*
Total Fat 0g	
Sodium 55mg	
Total Carb. 40g	0%
Sugars 40g	2%
Protein 0g	13%

Paying attention to the serving size and the number of servings in the container or package you're buying is very important. Only you can decide how much you eat or drink, but serving sizes can help you make smart choices.

Portion versus Serving Size

Sometimes people get the words portion and serving size mixed up. Both of them have to do with an amount of food you're eating.

You choose your portion size. It's the amount of food you choose to eat at a meal or in a snack. Serving sizes are amounts of food chosen by other people. Usually food companies come up with how big a serving size is, and they put that on food labels.

Look at food labels to figure out what the serving size of a particular food is. You'll find it near the top of the food label. All the rest of the nutrition information is based on that serving size.

Serving sizes aren't always based on how much people actually eat. A serving size also isn't always how much you *should* be eating. It depends on the food. If the serving size for some frozen broccoli is half a cup, you should definitely eat more! The more veggies the better. But a serving size of one ounce for a brownie is a guide you should stick to.

A portion of food might be the same as a serving size. A granola bar is probably one serving. You usually eat one granola bar at a time, so your portion is also one granola bar. If you eat two granola bars though, you're eating two servings.

Often, people end up eating way more than they need to. Their portions are just too big.

Keep in mind the more food you eat, the more calories you're taking in. Eating the right amount means getting the right number of calories. Eating big portion sizes all the time leads to weight gain pretty quickly.

What Do Portions Look Like?

So how are you supposed to know what healthy portions look like? One trick is to imagine portions of food as objects you already know.

- One cup of carrots is as big as a baseball.
- One-half cup of mashed potatoes is about as big as a light bulb.
- Two **ounces** of cheese are as big as four regular dice.

- One bagel should be as big across as a can of tuna.
- One waffle should be as big across as a CD.
- Three ounces of meat are as big as a deck of cards.
- One-quarter cup of nuts is as big as a golf ball.
- One brownie should be as big as a pack of dental floss.
- One muffin should be as big as a hockey puck.
- One cup of macaroni and cheese should be as big as a baseball.

What's an Ounce?

An **ounce** is a measure of weight. Ounces are bigger than grams. In fact, one ounce equals almost 30 grams. Sixteen ounces equals a pound.

What Are Food Groups?

We divide food up into **food groups** based on what kind of nutrients they have. The five food groups North Americans normally talk about are fruits, vegetables, grains, dairy, and protein (meat, beans, nuts). All dairy foods, for example, have some of the same nutrients. The dairy group is high in protein and calcium.

Do some research about what the right portion size for each kind of food is. Once you know that you should eat a cup of carrots, or two ounces of cheese, you can figure out what that looks like. Your family probably has some measuring cups and spoons around. Take a look at what a cup looks like. And a teaspoon. If you have a food scale, you can weigh out ounces. The more you know, the easier it will be to tell if you're eating the right portion.

Another way to imagine portions is to divide up your plate into **food groups**. Divide your plate into four equal sections, like you're cutting a pizza into four slices. One of the four sections is for a protein food, like meat or beans. Another section is for grains, like brown rice or whole-wheat pasta. The other two sections are for fruits and vegetables. Include a glass of milk on the side. The food you put on your plate shouldn't be piled too high and it shouldn't spill over into another section. You don't have to always eat like that, but it helps you figure out what a good amount of food to eat is.

Keeping Portions Under Control

Eating less might not sound like much fun. Won't you be hungry? Yes and no. People get used to eating so much, so they might think they're hungry when they make their portions smaller.

But really listen to your body. Try making your portions smaller and seeing what happens. You'll probably end up eating plenty of food, but you won't be feeling stuffed and bloated like you used to when you ate bigger portions all the time.

To eat smaller portions, try some different tricks. You can serve food on smaller plates and in smaller bowls. Imagine a sandwich on a huge dinner plate. Now picture it on a small plate. The sandwich looks bigger on the small plate. You actually will probably feel fuller if you eat it off the small plate. You'll be tricked into thinking you're eating more food. If you eat it off the huge plate, you'll think you didn't eat much food and will want more.

A History of Portions

Portions didn't use to be so big. Twenty years ago, people ate smaller portions. Bagels were three inches across. Today they are six inches across. Bigger bagels mean more calories. The three-inch bagels were 140 calories. Today, the average bagel is 350 calories. A cheeseburger used to be smaller, with 330 calories. Now cheeseburgers are a lot bigger, with 590 calories. We're eating more than we need to, and getting too many calories!

Instead of eating all the food on your plate as quickly as you can, take your time. It takes a few minutes for you to realize you're full, so eating slowly is the best way to keep from over-eating. Make sure to save the food you don't eat and have it later.

The Power of Good Habits

A habit is something you've done so many times that you keep doing it without having to think about it. For example, brushing your teeth every night before you go to bed might be a habit. You don't have to think about it—you just do it. Or a not-so-good habit might be chewing your fingernails when you feel nervous. It's something else you do without thinking.

Good habits can help you out a lot in life. They help you do things that are healthy for you every day, without giving them a thought. They make it easier to do healthy things.

We usually have to make an effort to make new habits—but once we've made a new habit, then we can stop thinking about it. Some scientists say that we need to do something for at least a couple of months before it will become a habit. That means you'll have to think about making a change in your life every day for at least two months. It won't be easy. But once you have a new habit, it will help you for the rest of your life!

Only take how much food you think you'll eat. Whether you're in the school lunch line or at home for dinner, don't pile your plate high out of habit. Pick just enough food that you'll eat. If you're still hungry when you're done with your first plate, take a little more food.

You don't always have to feel like you need to eat everything on your plate. And you don't have to throw out what you don't eat. You can always save some food for later in a reusable container. Even if you're at a restaurant, you can take your leftovers home. Then you can enjoy your meal twice!

Your family might want you to eat everything on your plate, though. They don't want you to waste food. And you shouldn't waste food! Explain to them you're trying to be healthier. And show them you won't waste food, you'll eat it later. Just be sure to follow up on your promise.

Many fast-food restaurants serve huge portions. One order of fries can be hundreds of calories, a big part of the total number of calories you need to eat in a day.

Don't skip meals either! Lots of young people skip breakfast because they don't have time to eat in the morning. Or lunch, because they forgot to bring one from home and they don't like school food.

Skipping meals sounds like eating less food. Actually, it ends up tricking you into eating more food. Think about it. You skip breakfast in the morning, so you are really, really hungry by lunchtime. You eat more than you normally would because you're so hungry. Besides your normal lunch, you also get a friend to give you half a sandwich and some chips. You buy ice cream and a soda from your cafeteria. In the end, you eat more than you would for breakfast and lunch combined!

Finally, eat slowly. People usually eat less when they eat slower. You could wolf down a huge plate of food in fifteen minutes. The better thing to do is to eat the same plate of food slowly. You'll realize you're full after a little while, and then you'll put down your fork. Then you can box up the rest and eat it later.

Portions at Fast-Food Restaurants

Fast-food restaurants are known for their huge portions. Endless sodas and buckets of fries as big as your head are the stars of the show. Big portions lead to big problems, though. Plus most fast foods are unhealthy anyway. Try to limit how much you eat. If you go to a fast-food place, order smaller sizes. Stay away from anything that says jumbo, extra large, gigantic, or super.

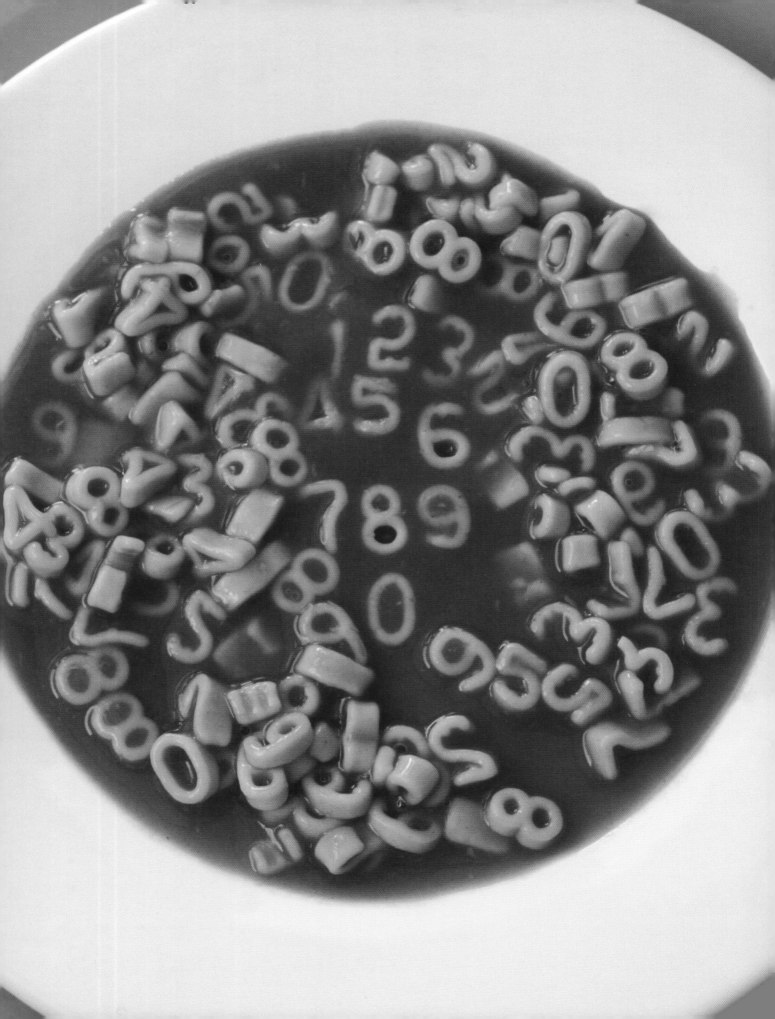

4

Keeping Track of the Numbers

Calories and portion sizes are just two numbers used to keep track of health. You can use numbers and math in other ways as well to keep track of your health. BMI and food and exercise diaries are all great ways to keep track of the numbers.

The Numbers of Weight

Weight already is a number. You weigh 80 or 100 or 150 or 200 pounds. And you can tell a little bit about your health by your weight. If you usually weigh 100 pounds, and then a month later you weigh 160, you know something is really wrong!

By itself, though, weight doesn't really tell you a lot. Everyone has a different healthy weight. Some people are naturally heavier or lighter. People with a lot of muscles weigh more than people without a lot of muscles. Even in one day, a person's weight changes because of what he ate and how much he exercised.

A better number is Body Mass Index (BMI). BMI is based on weight and height. Someone who weighs 120 pounds and is five feet tall is healthy. Someone who weighs 120 pounds but is three feet tall is overweight. And someone who is six feet tall and 120 pounds is underweight. Each person has a different BMI that tells whether he is a healthy weight or not.

You can find your BMI with an equation. First, weigh yourself and write it down. Then measure how tall you are in inches and write it down. Now you have to do a little math. The equation is:

$$BMI = weight \times 703 \div (height \times height)$$

First, multiply your weight by 703. Then multiply your height by itself. Last, divide the top number by the bottom.

Here's an example for someone who weighs 130 pounds and is four foot nine inches tall (57 inches):

BMI=130 pounds x 703 ÷ (57 inches x 57 inches)
BMI=91390 ÷ (57 x 57)
BMI=91390 ÷ 3249
BMI=28.1

So you have a BMI number. Now what? You can't do much with a BMI without a BMI chart. Doctors use charts to figure out if a BMI is healthy or not.

Doctors use two different BMI charts. One is for adults. One is for kids and teens ages two to nineteen. The charts are also divided into information for girls and boys. The charts help doctors figure out if their patients are underweight, overweight, obese, or a healthy weight.

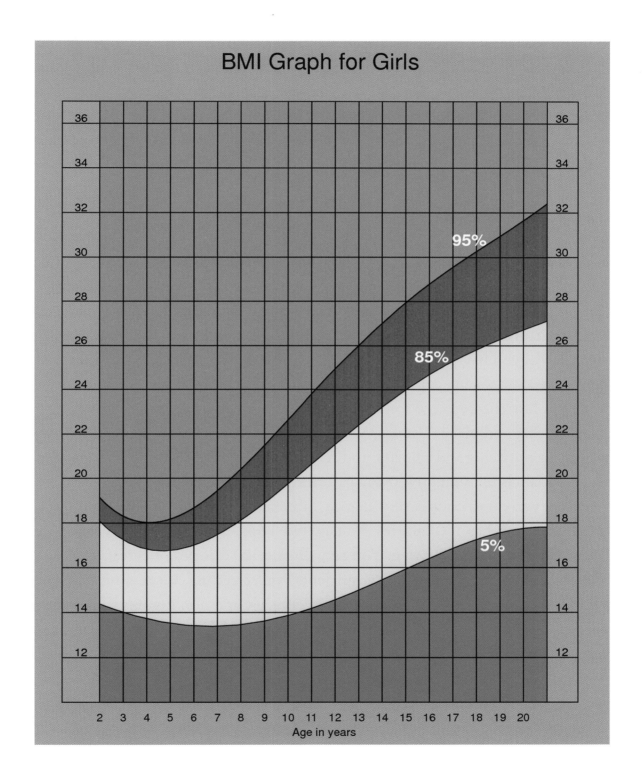

For young people, a BMI number is called BMI-by-age. The BMI number gets changed into something called a percentile. The percentile compares your BMI to everyone else's BMI who is also your age. A healthy BMI-by-age is between the fifth and eighty-fifth percentile.

BMIs can get confusing! Work with your doctor to figure out if you have a healthy BMI. If you find out you don't, you can also work with her to decide what to do about it. But don't decide you're overweight or underweight without talking to a doctor!

Food Diaries

Food diaries are a way to keep track of all the food you're eating. By keeping a food diary, you can see if you're getting enough nutrients and eating too many or too few calories.

Your goal is to write down everything you eat and drink in one day. Every meal and snack counts. You also have to write down the amounts of the food you eat. Try to guess how much cereal you have for breakfast—is it one cup? Two cups? You can measure it out to be sure. Use a measuring cup to portion out how much cereal you want to eat.

You have a few choices now for finding information about all the food you're eating. Food labels are a good place to start. Most foods in packages have food labels. You'll find the amounts of nutrients and calories you're eating right on the food's package.

First, food labels tell you how many calories you're eating. Make sure you know how many servings you eat to count every calorie. For example, a food label says one serving of cereal is one cup and has 150 calories. You ate two cups, which is two servings. You have to multiply the 150 calories by two. You actually ate 300 calories of cereal.

Food labels also tell you how many nutrients you're getting. Write down the nutrients for each food you eat. Use the daily value percentages, and don't worry about the grams and milligrams. However, you won't find daily values for sugar and protein, so write down how many grams of them are in your food. You'll also have to match the nutrients to the serving size. Again, if one serving of cereal has 15 percent of your daily value of vitamin A, ask yourself if you ate one serving. If you really ate two, multiply the 15 percent by two to get 30 percent.

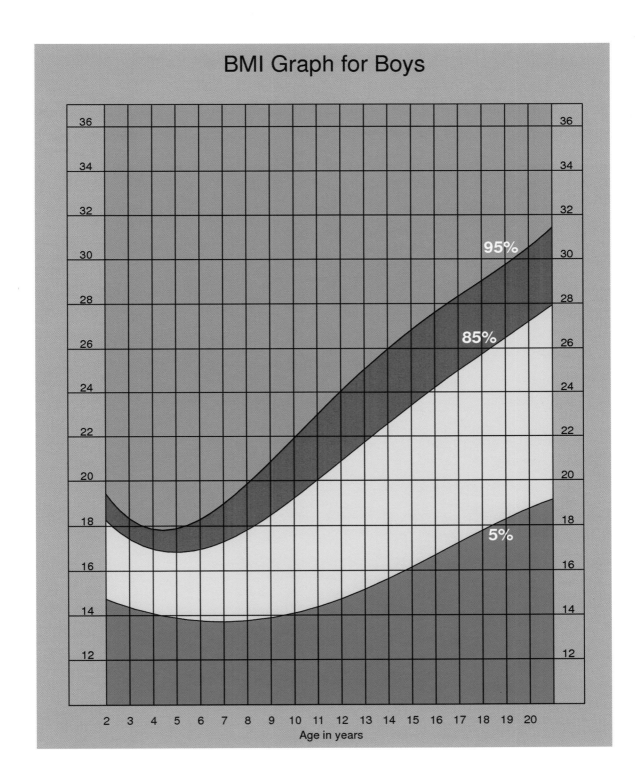

You can also check out websites that list thousands of foods' nutrition information. You need to know how much you ate of each food, and the website will tell you exactly how many calories and how many nutrients were in that food.

Make sure you don't change how you eat while you're keeping a food diary. Your goal is to see what your normal eating habits are like. Eating healthier just while keeping a

Keeping a food diary is a great way to make sure you're not eating more than you need. A food journal can help you see patterns in the foods you eat, too, which can help you to see if you need to change what you eat.

diary is cheating! Feeling guilty about what you're writing down might be a sign you know you should be eating healthier.

Now add everything up. Add up all the calories you ate in one day. Do they add up to around 2,000? They should. If you exercise a lot, more calories might be okay.

Do your daily values of nutrients add up to around 100 percent? When it comes to sugar, health experts say you shouldn't be eating more than 30 grams a day. Eating 30 grams of sugar or less a day is pretty healthy. For protein, you should be eating at least 40 to 50 grams a day. Younger people need a little less.

How did you do? Maybe you ate more calories than you needed. Or you didn't get enough vitamins. Or you ate too much sugar. Now you know where to start to change what you eat so you can be healthier.

You won't need to keep a food diary forever. It's just a tool to see how well you're eating. However, if you find you have poor nutrition, you might want to keep going with

Keeping Track of Exercise

Just like with food, you can also keep an exercise diary. Search for websites that list how many calories you burn doing different things. You'll need to type in your weight and how long you did an activity. Then you'll get a list of a bunch of activities and how many calories you burn doing each one. Keep a list of all the things you do during the day. You might start with "walk to school: fifteen minutes." Then you "sit: two hours." Followed by "basketball: forty minutes." And so on. Add up all the calories you burned to see how many extra calories you're burning in a day. (Remember, just living burns some calories.)

No matter what kind of sport, exercise, or outdoor activity you like, you're burning calories while doing it. Everything we do burns calories, but being active burns a lot more than sitting and watching TV. Getting up and getting outside, as well as eating right, is the best way to make sure you stay in shape.

your diary. The diary will help you make changes in what you eat, and you'll be able to see just how much better your **diet** gets. Of course, you'll also feel great when you eat healthier!

What's a Diet?

Your **diet** is all the food you eat. A healthy diet includes things like lots of fruits and veggies. The word diet can also mean a special way of eating to lose weight.

Find Out More

ONLINE

Exercise and Food Journal
www.kidsfoodjournal.com

Kids Calories Calculator
pediatrics.about.com/library/bl_calorie_calc.htm

KidsHealth: BMI charts
kidshealth.org/parent/growth/growth/bmi_charts.html

KidsHealth: Calories
kidshealth.org/kid/nutrition/food/calorie.html

Portion Size Plate
www.webmd.com/diet/healthtool-portion-size-plate

IN BOOKS

Edwards, Hazel and Goldie Alexander. *Talking About Your Weight*. New York: Gareth Stevens Publishing, 2010.

Nissenberg, Sandra K. *The Everything Kids' Cookbook*. Avon, Mass.: F+W Media, 2008.

McCarthy, Rose. *Food Labels: Using Nutrition Information to Create a Healthy Diet*. New York: Rosen Publishing, 2008.

Index

About the Author & Consultant

Kyle A. Crockett is a freelance writer whose work can be found in print and online. His writing for young people has focused on topics ranging from health to economics.

Dr. Borus graduated from the Harvard Medical School and the Harvard School of Public Health. He completed a residency in Pediatrics and then served as Chief Resident at Floating Hospital for Children at Tufts Medical Center before completing a fellowship in Adolescent Medicine at Boston Children's Hospital. He is currently an attending physician in the Division of Adolescent and Young Adult Medicine at Boston Children's Hospital and an Instructor of Pediatrics at Harvard Medical School.

Picture Credits